CALIFORNIA
ITS COAST AND DESERT

Sand dunes, Death Valley National Monument.

CALIFORNIA
ITS COAST AND DESERT

BY ROBERT REYNOLDS

TEXT BY RUTH KIRK AND ARCHIE SATTERFIELD

CALIFORNIA
ITS COAST AND DESERT

International Standard Book Number 0-912856-13-0
Library of Congress Catalog Number 74-75123
Copyright© 1974 by Publisher • Charles H. Belding
Graphic Arts Center Publishing Co.
2000 N.W. Wilson • Portland, Oregon 97209 • 503/224-7777
Designer • Robert Reynolds
Text • Archie Satterfield and Ruth Kirk
Printer • Graphic Arts Center
Binding • Lincoln & Allen
Printed in the United States of America
Second Printing

Sunset near San Simeon.

Mud hills at Zabriskie Point, Death Valley. ☐ Barrel cactus, Providence Mountains.

Aliso Beach.

THE COAST

TEXT BY ARCHIE SATTERFIELD

We waited until autumn to revisit the California coast, and it was late afternoon that September day when we wound down the Siskiyou Mountains along the Smith River and into the redwoods. The Smith was placid now in the tan and green stillness of autumn, the floods of winter yet to come. A soft haze drifted upstream from the ocean, muting the sunlight and giving the atmosphere a subtle odor and taste from the sea.

It is not an easy drive down the tortuous highway that seems to follow the river's every whimsical bend, but Jedediah Smith, for whom the river and a state park are named, had no easy journeys into the West, either. During his short life—he died at 33, a victim of Comanches along the Santa Fe Trail—he rang up a number of impressive firsts: He was the first to reach California by the Overland Route; to cross the Great Salt Lake Desert; to cross the Sierra Nevada, and he discovered the South Pass through the Rockies. But he was not a prolific diarist, and apparently so somber of personality that he has rebuffed those after-the-fact writers in search of charismatic heroes from the American frontier.

So it pleased us that a state park with 18 beautiful groves of redwoods near Crescent City were named for him. A giant among explorers—some believe more daring than Lewis and Clark and with a contribution to the westward movement of equal importance—it is only befitting that some of the tallest trees in the world bear his name.

Redwoods have many effects on those who look up to them. Some men calculate how many tabletops, houses and fence posts a single tree would produce. But we were there to appreciate, not calculate, and the usual adjectives one uses to describe anything big and beautiful become puny. How does one describe the tallest living thing? How can one comprehend something so huge growing from a seed only slightly larger than the head of a pin? How can one describe the silence that permeates a redwood grove when it is much more than the absence of sound; when it is a silence that reduces conversation to a respectful whisper used during religious ceremonies? For visiting a redwood grove and looking and savoring what you see and hear can be akin to a religious peace of mind.

There is another factor we considered while standing beside the Smith River and watching the slow water drift past the redwoods: Man is the only creature that apparently is capable of enjoying them aesthetically and emotionally, and the only creature that destroys them.

They are a remarkable form of life, a living fossil, a band of giants that once roamed the earth. They lived in Europe, in China and traces of them have been found on St. Lawrence Island in the Arctic and across North America. Now they are confined to the narrow coastal strip of California, a small tip of southwestern Oregon and a small area in Central China. In this country, only about 1.5 million acres of redwoods remain, and only about 235,000 acres of that is virgin, mostly in Humboldt and Del Norte Counties. Had it not been for dedicated conservationists nearly three-quarters of a century ago who formed the *Sempervirens Club* (the coast redwood is the *Sequoia sempervirens;* the Sierra redwood, decidedly different, is the *Sequoiadendron giganteum*), followed by the Save-the-Redwoods League, the coast redwood would have no virgin stands today. The Sierra redwoods got an earlier boost from conservationists when in 1864, President Lincoln signed a bill creating the first state park in the nation, protecting those in Yosemite Valley and Mariposa Grove, in central California.

The two giant trees differ in various ways, first of all by each refusing to grow in the other's environment. The coast redwood requires the summer fog and heavy rainfall of winter. The Sierra form thrives on extremes in temperature and a dry, fog-free climate.

To the casual eye, the major difference is one of appearance. The coastal giant grows rapidly; two and a half feet a year is common, and it tops off at over 300 feet under good growing conditions, its lowest branches a hundred feet above the forest floor. Its root system is shallow and when winter floods wash soil over its roots, a new set grow farther up the trunk.

The reddish bark is soft, virtually fireproof and impervious to boring insects. Its wood is highly resistant to rot and termites, its grain is straight. It reproduces primarily by sprouting, and several circular stands of the trees are the result of sprouts ringing a stump.

The Sierra giant has a thicker base, deeper fluting in the bark, its wood is of little commercial value because it is brittle, and it reproduces only from seed. It also lives up to 4,000 years, twice as long as its coastal cousin.

But statistics have a way of reducing the impact of a natural wonder, of removing the mystery that often is more pleasing to us because without statistics, our imagination can function in freedom; we can develop myths and legends that often are much more comforting than unemotional fact.

It is true that redwoods are a remnant of the age of giants but sentimentality over things past, causes and events beyond the reach of man's experience, serves no practical function. Everything on this planet does not have to be understood, dissected and stripped of its personality.

We thought of these things while traveling through the redwoods, and another, disquieting, thought came to us: Only after other giants of planetary antiquity diminished in size or disappeared only to leave their signature in skeletons and fossils; only after these things died or were dying, did man begin flourishing.

Why, we wondered, should all these things happen? Could not man exist among such giants? Was the climate such on the planet that man could not exist at all? Although there probably is no scientific evidence to prove that this Pythagorian leveling was anything other than coincidence, it leads one to wonder why giants and a creature as small as man could not coexist.

But this group of redwoods managed to hold out and thrive in this land of frequent fog and heavy rain, of moderate temperature, and of diversity within a relatively rigid structure of soil, climate and meteorological conditions.

When the first white men began cutting them into lumber, people in other parts of the country refused to believe such a tree existed and dismissed the evidence of their size as a tall tale out of the West.

At one time there were more than 300 sawmills in Del Norte, Humboldt and Mendocino Counties. The thick, fibrous bark was sold as home insulation and used in air conditioning.

Obviously, redwoods are not the only living thing along the Redwood Coast, but their bulk and height dictates that other plants in the same forest must contend with a life of little direct sunlight and thrive on rain and fog.

Thus, salal, thimbleberry, salmonberry, azalea, rhododendrons, fern and—watch your step—poison oak all give variety to the forest floor and add dashes of color as the mild seasonal changes occur. The seasonal changes are so subtle and so much alike that often the color changes are the only evidence available: It has been said that you need a calendar to tell the Fourth of July from Christmas. This condition is dominant in other forests along the California Coast, such as on Point Lobos, where spring plants emerge in the Christmas season.

The gentle giants also allow coexistence with numerous other species of trees. They share the land with Douglas fir, tanoak, madrone, maples, red alder, California laurel, California buckeye, Oregon oak, California black oak, western dogwood, Sitka spruce (in the northern reaches only), coast hemlock and Port Orford cedar.

We were unable to spend as much time in the redwoods as we wanted. How much time is enough in such a magnificent setting? We have never found the answer. To enjoy them thoroughly, and to explore most of the groves, we thought two weeks might be sufficient. But it is always wise, whether visiting a beautiful setting or a friend, to leave before you want to.

After Eureka we swung inland from the coast to the Avenue of Giants and wondered, as we wound along the highway through the trees, how we would react to the scenery if we suffered from claustrophobia. And we wondered if, since we were traveling the coast, if we shouldn't have turned on the less heavily used road and gone through Ferndale, Capetown, Petrolia, Upper Mattole, Honeydrew and Ettersburg—towns with gracious, casual-sounding names that appeared more directly related to the coast then Pepperwood, Weott, Garberville and the others.

Obviously we were not thinking in broad terms, and were not taking into consideration the whole coastal slope as a total environment. We did not think of the redwoods as being dependent on the ocean, the streams that feed into it or the climatic conditions the ocean creates. We were thinking of the parts, not the whole.

Our major disappointment, one we think justified and is shared by many Californians, is that the Avenue of the Giants, heavily advertised as it is, made us feel like Lilliputians hacking away at noble Gullivers whose only crime was being big and in the way. The Avenue, a section of old Highway 101, ambles around, among and between some magnificent stands of ancient redwoods, some so close to the highway that they have been nicked by trucks and campers, a testament to their hardiness and the thickness of their bark.

Not once were we beyond the sound of the traffic. Later we were told that a freeway was begun through them, which resulted not only in many trees being felled, but also in unstable soil conditions and unnatural drainage patterns that threatened those left living.

The Save-the-Redwoods League, the Sierra Club and other groups forced a moratorium on the freeway construction through Prairie Creek State Park. The freeway route, at this writing, is in a limbo while the conservationists continue their attempt to save the redwoods by pointing out that there are other uses for public funds than building more freeways when gasoline no longer is considered an infinite resource.

We had lost the coast and were anxious to rejoin it when we reached Leggett and Highway I. We turned off 101 and dipped and swerved and climbed and braked our way downward to the sea again.

Although friends had described the Mendocino Coast to us as still open, pastoral land, after an absence of several years we were certain it had become a vast housing development. We did not believe the most populous state in the nation could have mile after mile of rural and seemingly untouched land remaining. We were certain the California Coastal Alliance had won an empty victory when in 1972 the Coastal Zone Conservation Act was approved by voters.

We were pleasantly surprised. The Mendocino Coast remains.

The towns that look so large on maps are tiny. Cattle still graze beside the highway. The land still soars gently upward from the sea, open meadows punctuated by oak trees reminding one of African plains minus prides of lions dozing beneath the shade at noon.

The Mendocino Coast does not look like a coast in many places. That may seem a contradiction, but when one associates a coastline with long sand dunes, battered offshore rocks and wide, sandy beaches, the Mendocino seems gentle and subtle by comparison. Grazing land undulates downward to the sea, and grapestake and redwood fences, invariably in need of repair it seems, give the coastline a feeling of unpretentiousness.

There is an absence of artsy-craftsy, Ye Olde English geegaw stores, elegant service stations and motels and condominiums dominating the views. After hearing so much about the artists attracted to the coast, we expected the town of Mendocino to be cute. Instead, we found it and its neighboring towns to be rather honest and straightforward in appearance. If artists are moving in, they are unobtrusive as true artists are, rather than turning the towns into sandwich boards for their presence.

Although we were aware of the battle over the coastal conservation measure, we were relieved that the matter had been settled by voters in favor of regulation. When one finds an area as beautiful as the Mendocino Coast, you wonder how it could possibly be improved upon. If other stretches of the coast are considered examples of improvement, our vote would be definitely in favor of the status quo.

For the naturalist, no part of the Mendocino Coast is more interesting than the pygmy forests along its staircase plateaus. Here the sea was the creator. Broadly speaking, the level of the sea rose and fell as the water was repeatedly locked up, then released as the great glaciers of the last Ice Age expanded and retreated. In addition, the level of the land itself has shifted. As a result the changing sea level has cut its signature on the coast with a series of steps notched on the land, each level roughly 100,000 years older as one climbs, and each about 100 feet above the other.

The sand dunes of the present beach are on the lowest and most recent level. The sand has been stabilized by thick-leafed salt and drought-resistant plants such as the silver-colored Franseria and the yellow verbena. They crawl over the dunes, anchoring themselves as they move along and drop long, moisture-seeking roots. They are hardy in terms of natural elements but sensitive to trampling. When the plants no longer anchor the sand, the dunes begin moving onto vegetated soil, killing grass, isolating and then smothering trees. The moving sand can slowly but relentlessly kill a lake.

We can learn from the fate of Africa's desert. In Kenya, for example, the desert advances six miles a year into the forest and in a recent 300-year period the Sahara advanced 250 miles north on a 1,250-mile front, turning 390,000 acres into a wasteland. While we, in our technological security and ability to learn from the past, say we can control such things, we should always remember that such things are not always controlled until the crisis stage is reached or passed.

On the second and third levels of the staircase is a rich forest community. Douglas fir, grand fir, hemlock and redwood share this level. Also here, near Caspar, is the first appearance of Sitka spruce, a tree whose range follows the coastline far into Alaska to the edge of the treeless tundra. Other trees, which grow owing to the stabilization of sand, include the Bishop pine and the shore pine. The Bishop pines are closely related to the Monterey pines farther south, and they are rare today compared with the vast forests they once composed. Only isolated stands of them survive, scattered almost at random from Baja California to the Mendocino Coast. Their cones have been found in the La Brea tar pits in Los Angeles' Hancock Park beside skeletons of mammoths and sabre-toothed tigers.

The cones develop early as pines go, sometimes as early as the tree's fifth or sixth year, first growing on the trunk, then forming circles around main branches. The Bishops are the "fire type" pines that require intense heat of forest fires to produce the opening of the cones and let the seeds fall to the ashy soil.

The next step of 100,000 years upward is one of the least vegetated on the staircase. Few redwoods grow this high and nutrients have been leached from the soil by rainfall that sinks down to the hardpan, then flows laterally to the next lower level. At this upper level again is found the Bishop pine mixed among the wax myrtle and the chinquapin.

The higher terraces are underlain by patches of hardpan that collect water to form bogs, which in turn support separate plant communities that include the Canadian dogwood, sphagnum moss and the jeweled sundew. The sundew traps insects with its sticky bristles to add nutrients lacking in the virtually sterile soil.

Scattered along the terraced coastline are pygmy forests tucked in among the giant redwoods and other trees. The most famous such forest is at the Institute of Man in Nature on Jug Handle Creek near Caspar. The institute was formed in 1968 and hopes to acquire some 600 acres for a total ecological community. The project has been partially successful by having the area declared the Pygmy Forest National Landmark, and the institute has acquired a portion of the 600 acres.

A major force behind the institute is John Olmstead, who leads four-hour hikes through the forest every Sunday morning during the summer. He tells his groups that the staircase along Jug Handle Creek is the only place he knows where, in one day, you can learn so much about the formation of the Pacific coast. Here one can see some of the tallest redwoods in existence, while growing virtually beside them are miniature versions of the same redwoods, shorter than a tall man. It gives one the disquieting feeling he is looking at the same object but through opposite ends of a pair of binoculars.

Olmstead's lecture-hike turns the staircase into a map of natural history spanning half a million years, beginning at the 400,000-year level and ending four miles and three steps later at the present.

The Pygmy forest is on the third level, and the normal cypresses and pines disappear. An 80-year-old evergreen tree is only a few inches over six feet. Under normal growing conditions it would be at least 80 feet tall.

Olmstead's punch line on the soil tells the entire story:

"This soil is as strong as household vinegar. It is about the most acidic in the world."

The rock-hard, impenetrable layer of clay keeps moisture from seeping down during the rainy winter, and it also keeps tree roots from searching out water tables below. As a result roots nearly drown in the winter and parch in summer.

It is a harsh condition, but the pygmy forest is an extremely stable ecosystem, and almost indestructible. The only way to change it, apparently, is to break down the hardpan clay.

Short-term versus long-term benefits is a popular phrase among planners and environmentalists, and nowhere is it more apparent than on the gentle, foggy, pastoral Mendocino Coast. Caught in the middle, as usual, are the landowners who can easily be forced out by rising property taxes.

In spite of the Coastal Zone Conservation Act, there is a chain of events that occurs in land transactions as inevitable as the winter fog. Farming and ranching on a family basis are giving way everywhere to corporate farming and feedlots. Smaller farmers and ranchers, unable to compete, also are unable to pay the steadily increasing taxes on their holdings. They sell at the highest price they can get. The land and neighboring land then is assessed upward to reflect the sale price. Only land developers can afford to buy the land. Then it is broken up into lots, sold for second or retirement homes. County governments, faced with a dwindling tax base due to lack of industry, also are faced with increasing costs. The circle becomes tighter. Someone or something must suffer. Usually it is that indefinable concept known as the quality of life.

Basically, what brings about this unpleasant chain of events is an inarticulate emotion that attracts each of us to the coastline. Love of the sea is universal. Some believe that the attraction is something transmitted down the millennia through our genes. Combine this with the highly developed sense of personal property in America and the coast becomes the victim. It is loved to death, much like a child in a bitter divorce case.

Most of us participate in this paradox of land use and ownership. While we decry the loss of public access to beaches and headlands, we also yearn for our own private bluff with a secluded beach below. It is not so much for the pride of ownership (although status symbols cannot be overlooked) as it is the desire to have a private place where nobody can reach us. It is the same need that drives us farther and farther into the wildernesses of the world when we have time off from our city jobs. Psychologists probably say this is a manifestation of the desire to return to those wonderful secret places we had as a child. The philosopher and the realist say it is impossible. Yet, to many of us, the epitome of ownership is to have a home facing the sea and the setting sun. Thus, the dilemma of the coast.

The Mendocino Coast had one more pleasant interlude for us. We had seen no fog. The days had been clear, as we were told only September can promise. We had watched Highway I unwind ahead of us and had seen everything in a photographic clarity. Yet we wanted at least a trace of fog to assure us it occurred as advertised.

Then we crested the hill high above Russian Gulch State Park, and pulled to the shoulder of the highway and climbed a low hill. Far below we could see the highway and the numerous switchbacks that took it down the barren mountainside before

flattening out at the gulch, only to begin climbing again on the far side.

Then we saw the fog. It came in from the sea in streamers as the warm air met cooler land air. Each streamer would dart inland a short distance, then disappear beneath the sun, its place soon taken by another streamer. But they were unable to unite into a fog bank. The sun withstood the attack.

It is unfashionable for protectors of nature to like highways. In the case of freeways, it is easy to understand because, as that great California writer, John Steinbeck, said of freeways: It is possible to drive all the way across the nation without seeing a single thing.

But we were enchanted with Highway I. It is undoubtedly the most beautiful highway we have traveled. It is crooked, potentially dangerous, tiring if one drives too long, and seems to consist of a series of blind curves and hills as sharp at the top as a ski-lodge roof. But it possesses a masculine grace as it follows the contours of the shoreline, soaring across ravines on delicate bridges, swerving around coves and plunging in and out of groves of timber. It was built in those leisurely pre-freeway days when driving was an act of pleasure.

It was late afternoon when we were just north of Bodega Bay. A light rain started falling and we stopped at a viewpoint to watch the mist move in, the sunlit mountains becoming dappled, then gray as the rain moved inland. Across the cove from us stood a line of cars, the owners below in inflatable boats ending a day of scuba diving. They deflated the boats, packed them into the cars and the lights flicked on.

Before the lights went on, the cars blended into the darkening landscape, but with the headlights on and the cars beginning to back out, they took on a science-fiction appearance. It looked as though we were the last living things on the coast and only machines were moving about all around us. Then we remembered that any phenomenon, natural or technological, can take on any personality we give it. I started the motor, turned on the headlights, flicked the turn indicator, put the automatic transmission in drive, released the brake, depressed the accelerator, turned the steering gear and fell into line with the motorists heading home for San Francisco.

We had one more stop to make before San Francisco, and that would be Point Reyes National Seashore—earthquake country, land of almost constant wind. The windswept peninsula long has been a favorite spot for naturalists and through efforts of the Sierra Club and other organizations it was preserved as a park. Today, about a half of the 53,000 acres allotted to the park remain in private ownership, and the public land is divided into two areas for visitors.

The peninsula catches the worst of storms that come to the area, often collecting 55 inches of rainfall a year. On an annual basis, the wind velocity is more than 20 miles an hour, and for one six-day period, the wind blew 50 miles an hour. During one wild 24-hour period, the wind averaged 80 miles an hour, and the peak reached was 120 miles an hour.

Here, too, the Bishop pine grows, frequently laden with green moss and lichens. One is seldom out of sound of the surf that thunders against the peninsula's walls and sweeps the beaches dotted around the cliff bottoms.

The peninsula is slowly being separated farther from the mainland by the famous San Andreas Fault, and it was here that the greatest movement of earth occurred during the 1906 earthquake that destroyed San Francisco. The largest single land movement was 20 feet, where the Sir Francis Drake Highway ended abruptly, then picked up again 20 feet away.

The headquarters of the National Seashore are at the old Skinner Ranch. There, the ground moved 15 feet in front of the ranch house and a garden path that once led to a door suddenly ended against a wall. A self-guiding Earthquake Trail has been laid out—the only one in the nation—with signs pointing out reminders of the 1906 quake; a fence that moved 15 feet, a creek bed that was changed, a spot where a cow was swallowed up in a fissure with only its tail left above ground.

Geologists continue to study the point, which moves seaward at an average rate of two inches a year, and most believe the San Andreas fault and its movement is the best laboratory for studying the theory that continents once were connected.

In all, the place had a dark, gloomy beauty to it on the day of our visit, making it easy to believe that Sir Francis Drake did, indeed, select what is now known as Drake's Bay rather than San Francisco Bay to career, repair and refit his vessel, the *Golden Hind,* in June, 1579. The history of those early voyages makes for reading that is at once exciting and gloomy: scurvy, lashings, casual cruelty on shore and aboard the ship.

The fog was a complete cover when we left, then disappeared as we climbed back toward Highway 101 and drove south across the Golden Gate Bridge, through San Francisco and down through the Santa Cruz Mountains to our next rendezvous.

Many years ago when I first visited the Monterey Peninsula as a sailor, I was fortunate in my reading material before the visit. I had never heard of the place. My reading material peaked out with books by Richard Halliburton and other adventurers of the day, and I had never heard of John Steinbeck or Robinson Jeffers, and probably wouldn't have read them if I had. Henry Miller was a faintly familiar name but his "good" books were safely imprisoned in Europe and some ministers said nations that allowed such books to exist deserved World War II.

So I first visited this literary coast through my own senses. Compared with the conservative, stolid Midwest I came from, the Navy-oriented San Diego where I spent four years, the sprawl of Los Angeles and the sophistication of San Francisco, the Monterey area had a hard-working, direct, yet warm feel to it. Our ship anchored far out to sea and those of us who wanted liberty had to ride the dory-type liberty launches through heavy groundswells into Monterey Bay. The trip was so rough that one young seaman went AWOL, caught a bus to San Diego and was waiting on the dock when we returned. Nobody really blamed him. The trip was made in sunlight with a following sea; the return against a strong headwind that sliced off the tops of the swells and threw them into the boat.

But most of us remembered Monterey as a place of good jazz in the bars and good conversation among the locals. Most of us wanted to return and spend a week; few of us did.

Since then my education on the Monterey Peninsula has increased, vicariously perhaps, but from good teachers; the novels and stories of Steinbeck, the craggy and often nihilistic poetry of Robinson Jeffers, and a brief friendship with a veteran of several years of living on Anderson Creek in Big Sur before it was the fashionable thing to do. Each of these gave me a feeling that the bay and the Big Sur coast were familiar grounds.

The Monterey Peninsula, for the casual visitor, is a great place to load up with guide books, a pair of binoculars, camera, plant and bird guides, picnic lunches and comfortable walking shoes. In spite of its perpetual danger of being loved to death, it, like memories from youth, manages to remain intact.

We were about a month early for the great monarch butterfly migration to Pacific Grove. Having seen the distinctive black-and-orange insects in other parts of the country, including one high in the Coast Range near Chilkoot Pass in Alaska, they were no stranger to us. But there apparently is no other place quite like Pacific Grove for the insects with habits as set as those of a salmon. In spite of the increasing population and the number of people who walk out to Point Pino to stare at them, the monarchs keep arriving each October, earlier if a hard winter is due, then return North about March. While no accurate count can be taken, population estimates range up to two million at a time wintering there.

They come singly, in groups of two or three or in a dark cloud just above wave tops, threading among fishing boats offshore, on their way from Alaska, British Columbia and the Pacific Northwest states. When the migration reaches its peak, they will fly through mountain passes in a steady stream that may take two days or more to complete. This homing instinct is so strong that storms may blow them aside several miles, but never off course. They will fly over forest fires rather than around, fluttering steadily upward until they are over the heat.

Stops for food and rest are infrequent.

This direct-route navigation often grounds them at the north end of Monterey Bay when fog and mist blocks the route. But when the sun returns, they lift off in vast flocks and flutter onward to the Monterey pines, locally called the "butterfly trees," the only trees they will winter in.

Into three acres these tens of thousands of insects set up their winter quarters. They close their wings and sit or hang from the lichen, needles or bare branches, looking like masses of brown leaves.

For the first few days after their arrival, the sojourners are still tense and restless. They flutter nervously, feed often, take off in alarm in spinning masses. Gradually they settle into their winter routine.

They are quite safe from birds; apparently they taste terrible. The few reported cases of a bird snatching one from the sky are usually followed by a vigorous spitting out. Infrequently, very infrequently, a bird will eat one, but one must assume it is a hungry bird that does so.

Sometimes during a cool night the monarchs lose their hold on the pines and fall harmlessly to the ground to be revived by the morning sun. On those rare occasions when the thermometer drops drastically, the butterflies freeze and form deep carpets beneath the trees like autumn in New England.

But monarchs are remarkably durable. Rain has no effect on them; it runs off their folded wings. When a gale hits the coast, they move to the lee side of the pines and hang on. Those blown away either hide in crevices on the ground, or for days come straggling in after the storm.

Their migratory paths and navigational apparatus remain a mystery, but there is evidence that they, like bees and ants, use polarized light for a guide. It is known that they do not migrate in cloudy weather.

Pacific Grove has both capitalized on the butterflies and gone to great lengths to protect them. Chamber of Commerce festivals are held in the butterflies' honor, but it also is a $500 fine and jail sentence for molesting the monarchs.

The Monterey Peninsula is best known to Americans as the home country of John Steinbeck, and many mistakenly assume that everyone there speaks that poetic Spanish-American language of *Cannery Row, Tortilla Flat, Sweet Thursday* and his other Monterey books. One cannot drive through the valleys behind the peninsula and outside Salinas without remembering his stories of the farmers and the workers, and when one comes back to the coast, the grandfather in *Red Pony* tells us again that "westering" has died out and that the West Coast is lined with old men with no place to go.

Steinbeck's raw materials are still there: The cannery buildings, a Chinese grocery store, a marine research laboratory, and a general atmosphere of hard-working and hard-playing still thrive in the towns.

We left the peninsula cities and went into Robinson Jeffers country. And Point Lobos held no surprises. Jeffers had written of its wildness so convincingly that the calm day we had there was almost a disappointment. We wanted a storm like the one we had on Point Reyes. We wanted to sit in a gale and read Jeffers' words, to see them brought to life.

Point Lobos epitomizes Jeffers' poetry and we associate the point with his aloof, angry, dark reading of human destiny. The point embodies his belief that nature is permanent; that man is doomed to destruction, and that civilization, even though responsible for saving the point from destruction, is still transient: Jeffers believed that mankind's destiny was to despoil nature, then pass into oblivion, leaving the unchanging nature alone again.

Man could live on Point Lobos, but to what purpose? The preservation of this 400-odd acres in its natural state is proof that, while we may be sometimes as bad as Jeffers thought, we still are capable of responsible acts.

Here lives the Monterey cypress. Here, too, are 176 species of vertebrates, 88 marine invertebrates, 10 amphibian and reptiles, 19 mammals, 147 varieties of birds, and at least 300 varieties of plants. Of all these life forms, the one that symbolizes Point Lobos is the cypress. Contorted by the harsh environment, its branches sometimes are stripped barren of foliage but are coated with a form of red algae which looks something like melted wax.

The cypress once was widely distributed along the coast, but now grow only on Point Lobos and Cypress Point in their natural state. It joins the redwood, the sequoia, the Bishop pine, the Torrey pine near San Diego, the Catalina ironwood and the dwarf Gowen cypress near Monterey as remnants from another time, still holding stubbornly to existence.

The wind-tortured cypresses usually have swollen and misshapen bases and are a favorite for photographers and artists as frames for photos of the rocky surf below.

Strangely, they thrive in less hostile areas and make excellent windbreaks due to their rapid growth. But they do not usually live long away from their native, harsh coast. It is as though a milder, sedentary life is not good for this species.

Point Lobos has been called "the greatest meeting of land and water in the world," a definition first uttered by a painter, Francis McComas. Those who like other stretches of coastline might argue the point since any visit to the shore is subjective. Still there is no denying that Point Lobos is a powerful place to visit, and if Robert Louis Stevenson was moved to use Whaler's Knoll as the genesis of *Spyglass Hill,* and naturalists from all over America fought for its preservation, why argue with one person's love of the area? Enjoy, enjoy.

As we entered that stretch of coastline known as the Big Sur Coast, natural history then shared our consciousness with memories of a friendship a few years ago. For Big Sur is as important to American art and letters as it is to natural history. It was known in post-World War II days as something of a Shangri-La for artists and writers, and judging from what its early residents say about it, Big Sur was one of those special places that exist for a brief period in a state of simplicity before some residents leave and others arrive with different ideas about how a community of artists should live.

Everything changes, though, and whether the changes are for good or ill depend on the person one talks to. Some traces of the original free style of life remain. There is no organized chamber of commerce at Big Sur, but those who write to the chamber receive replies from volunteers in the community. Community matters are discussed and settled in the Big Sur Grange Hall, where potluck suppers and parties are held and movies are shown. As with the rest of the world, the population is more transient today.

Anderson Creek was very much in our minds as we drove through the village, still cleaning up from a massive landslide in 1972. There were two early residents of the Big Sur artists colony shortly after World War II that made the place important to us—Henry Miller and Hugh O'Neill.

I knew the latter personally and admired his philosophy; I admired the former's literary output, and through Miller's writing became acquainted with Big Sur and O'Neill.

O'Neill spent several years on Anderson Creek and when I knew him, he spoke of it simply as an interesting period he had lived through. He found being a POW in Germany interesting rather than brutal (and it was brutal for him), and this capacity to accept experience he made Big Sur more important for me than it had been before.

We worked in the same office and lived in the same neighborhood and formed a car pool on an occasional basis. A tall, slender man with a shock of white hair, horn-rimmed glasses and a soft, cultivated voice, he attracted people without effort. O'Neill was noted for his intelligence and the ability to care deeply about something without being a bore.

His years at Big Sur shortly after World War II that intrigued us the most, and I remember those conversations more vividly than his stories published in British magazines.

He told about moving into the cabins that were built for the convicts who worked on Highway I before World War II. He told of planting a large vegetable garden, and he spoke of the

fog with a sense of wonder; how those who lived low in the fog belt could raise certain types of fruit and vegetables, and those above the fog raised other types. He told of walking up and down the steep mountainside in and out of the fog, and of the two-world feeling it gave him to leave the damp darkness of the fog and enter the dry, sun-lit world.

He talked of standing in one spot, a bluff, and playing shadow games with his body, the sun casting his shadow on the fog below.

He spoke of these things with his gentle wit, but seldom talked about the people there. When pressed, he said, "Yes, I built a porch for Henry Miller," and he told of another Big Sur resident, a self-destructive writer who published a fine war novel. But he never mentioned the fact that Henry Miller wrote with great warmth about one Hugh O'Neill in one of his books.

He was not a rabid activist; he was too polite for that. But there were certain things about our society in general and our office in particular he did not like. One day he was simply gone. I have no idea where he went, but I hope the present gives him as much pleasure and peace of mind as the past did. He is one of those rare people whose presence can enrich one's life. Men free of hate are difficult to find, and Hugh O'Neill is one of them.

During one of our conversations, O'Neill told me about the sea otter; introduced me to them, actually, because I have a tendency to take on my species of wildlife one at a time. He enchanted me with his stories of sitting on headlands and watching them play below. He is a gifted storyteller without the wild embellishments tinged with superstition associated with the Irish. Yet, I didn't completely take his word for it. Could there be such a beautiful animal, one of such sensitivity and good cheer, even after being slaughtered to the brink of extinction? Thankfully, there is. The otter is all the argument one needs to preserve living things from extinction: without the otter, life on this planet would be a little less tolerable for the rest of us.

We tried to erase it from existence. My, how we tried. First were the Russians, to whom the otter was more valuable than any gold that might be found. In fact, fur was so prominent in the plans of the Russians and to the officials of the British Hudson's Bay Company that employees were forbidden to search for gold. Gold would bring others to their territories, and greed for fur could not stand the competition of greed for gold.

So they systematically killed the sea otter, beginning with the rigorous discovery trip in 1741 by Vitus Bering. After his crew lived on otter meat that winter, and made shelters of their skins, they returned to Russia with more than 700 pelts. By 1804, some 15,000 pelts were being hauled to Russia in one ship. So vast was the slaughter that by 1818, Baron von Wrangell of the Russian-American Company warned that the otter would be extinct soon unless restrictions were made.

In the meantime, the Russians had established Fort Ross in 1812 as an outpost for the otter on the California coast because of the heavy concentration of the animal there. The fort passed into private ownership after the Russians left North America and it was used by ranchers for a variety of purposes, including the striking Russian Orthodox chapel, which collapsed in the 1906 earthquake. Shortly afterward, the California Historical Landmarks Committee of San Francisco bought the fort, then turned it over to the state as a park. The chapel burned in 1970, but a second restoration is planned.

But the slaughter of the sea otter continued in the early 19th Century, down the coast as far as San Francisco, and north to the Arctic Ocean. Hawaiians were kidnapped and brought to North America to dive in the ocean after otters that had been killed and sank, and Aleuts were brought from the Arctic to hunt them from their kayaks. Males, females and pups were killed, thousands wasted by shooting them from the beach and hoping they would wash ashore.

In 1911, a fleet of 31 schooners headed for the otters' big breeding ground in the Bering Sea, and came home with only about a dozen pelts. That same year the last pelt sold on the legitimate market in London brought $1,900. When it apparently was too late, the greed sated, England, Russia, Japan and the

United States agreed the otter should be protected, and it became a federal offense to own any part of an otter pelt in this country.

California passed a law giving the lovely creatures more protection. The year was 1913, the same year Pacific Grove passed a law protecting the monarch butterfly. But the otter apparently had abandoned the whole West Coast. It was believed that the only sea otters in existence were in their traditional breeding grounds in Alaskan waters.

There had been sightings in secluded coves, but in one case, people celebrating American independence dropped Fourth of July firecrackers down on the otters and they were never seen in that particular cove again.

Twelve years later, in 1925, a service station attendant fifteen miles south of Carmel at Bixby Creek, saw something in the surf he had never seen before. It obviously was not the sea lions that have always lived there, and were blessed with a less attractive pelt. The man called a game warden, who identified the creature as the sea otter, back from the edge of total extinction.

Their fur is perhaps the most beautiful of any mammal. Soft, satiny, it is so dense that it is almost impossible to reach the skin with one's fingers. It is extremely durable and ranges in color from brown to nearly black, with a delicate sprinkling of silver guard hairs.

Thus, grief, like affection, is not a purely human emotion. The grieving otter usually survived, as mothers do, and one wonders if their memories would be tainted for the remainder of their lives.

It is that warm, perky personality that makes sea otter so valuable to us. In 1742, that great naturalist who accompanied Bering, Georg Wilhelm Steller, wrote:

"They prefer to live together in families, the male and his mate, the half-grown young and the very young sucklings all together. The male caresses the female by stroking her, using the forefeet as hands; she, however, often pushes him away from her for fun and in simulated coyness, as it were, and plays with her offspring like the fondest mother. Their love for their young is so intense that when their young are taken away they cry bitterly, and grieve so much that after ten or fourteen days they grow as lean as skeletons and become sick and feeble and will not leave the shore."

Next to the penguin, there is no creature more fun to watch. They play constantly, flipping water in each others' eyes, tossing shells or wads of seaweed back and forth, standing erect treading water and holding one paw like a hand to shade their eyes.

They eat three meals a day, sometimes working a snack in between meals, diving for their food up to 150 feet deep. Their main course is abalone, but also eat cuttlefish, sea urchins and other bottom creatures. If they bring up a shellfish, they frequently will lay a flat rock on their belly and crack the shell on it.

When they sleep or nap, they wind themselves in kelp to keep from drifting away, and when they see a pod of killer whales coming their way, rather than heading for shore, they become motionless, like a log, and hope the whales will so mistake them.

Originally, this otter lived on land as its cousins still do and went to sea only for food and play. But at some point they became nearly amphibious creatures, and now make kelp beds their home.

It is a marvel of family life to watch them teach their young to swim. The pups are born knowing how to float on their back, but like infant humans, they do not like to be far from their mother. Often the mother, cradling the youngster on her belly, will wait until it falls asleep, then slowly sink from beneath it and stay nearby until it wakes. The mother thus teaches it how to swim and to be self-sufficient in the most gentle way possible. She wraps it in kelp when she dives for food and spends a great deal of time grooming both her pup and her own pelt. Even those who killed them for a living often admitted the otter was almost human in their personalities, and noted their generosity. For example, after one has dived to the bottom for a shellfish and a pounding rock, then surfaced to float on its back and bash

away for the goodies inside, another otter may swim over, grab the fresh food and casually eat it. The otter that did all the work simply dives again for another morsel and brings his bashing stone back up with him. No hard feelings.

So the otter has come back. They have been transplanted from Alaska to the Washington and Oregon coasts amid great welcoming fanfare, and their progress is watched intently by biologists and all who love a beautiful and playful animal.

To repeat, life on this planet would be a little less tolerable without them.

It was with some reluctance that we left the Big Sur Coast and the challenge of driving on Highway I. The narrow road gradually straightened out until we no longer were beneath the steep mountains. Suddenly, it seemed, Big Sur was behind us.

Another change we saw was the abundance of houses perched on the cliffs, in the coves and virtually suspended from the cliffs. Yet the purple haze of late afternoon, the fog, the sea otter, the redwoods and the steep Santa Lucia Range with its wilderness areas remain. While it may never match the Mendocino Coast's pristine quality, the beauty of the Big Sur will remain so long as the Coastal Zone Conservation Act is enforced.

Soon we were out of the rugged headlands and coves and onto the flat plateau over the sea that characterizes the highway to its southern end. We were reminded of parts of Colorado and Wyoming as we drove past the grazing land, brown now from the summer heat. And we could imagine how beautiful it would be in the spring when the rain brought out the greenery.

For a naturalist driving the coast north to south, the trip is ending at San Simeon. The open, untouched coast ends there and the realm of the architect, the developer, and the sociologist begins. From Santa Barbara south, the shore is a city; the surf a playground with property values dictated by the view, the proximity to beaches and boat basins.

We joined Highway 101 at San Luis Obispo, then swung back to the coast just north of Santa Barbara shortly before sunset. It was to be our last sunset on the coast because the sky was overcast during the remainder of our trip. The day turned red as the sun sank, giving the elegant stucco buildings of Santa Barbara a slight pink tint and turning the tile roofs almost black. Out in the channel a ship steamed slowly past the offshore drilling platforms that look like machinery yet to be invented on the surface of a planet yet to be discovered. The sun appeared to grow as it sank, and we stopped to watch the day end with the ship headed directly into the sun that rippled and shimmered, then disappeared. The palm trees became silhouettes and the white stucco held the last light of day when it seemed all light had gone.

It was a special moment. Although there were about 200 miles of coastline left to cover on this voyage of rediscovery, we had felt a sense of finality when Highway I merged with Highway 101. The wild coast, the natural coast was behind us.

As we drove through Los Angeles, followed the coastline south to San Diego and caught glimpses of the ocean between houses lining the beach, we understood why California has spawned so many individuals and organizations whose sole purpose is to preserve natural beauty. It was California's natural heritage that first came under the threat of extinction.

It is one of the great ironies of nature that the beautiful areas attract the most people, many of whom would never consider living in a less beautiful place. But the beauty that brings them is either trampled, altered or placed on the auction block.

California has had the reputation of being a national pacesetter in fashion, arts and letters and other fields. Now, with the Coastal Zone Conservation Act a viable force in state planning, that incredible coastline loved by Californians and other Americans has a much better chance of survival. The redwoods, the sea otter and the monarch butterfly, and now the entire coast, have been accorded a great measure of protection. This is adequate proof that those professional skeptics who say man is totally destructive are not totally correct.

There is always hope, and California has a coastline to prove it.

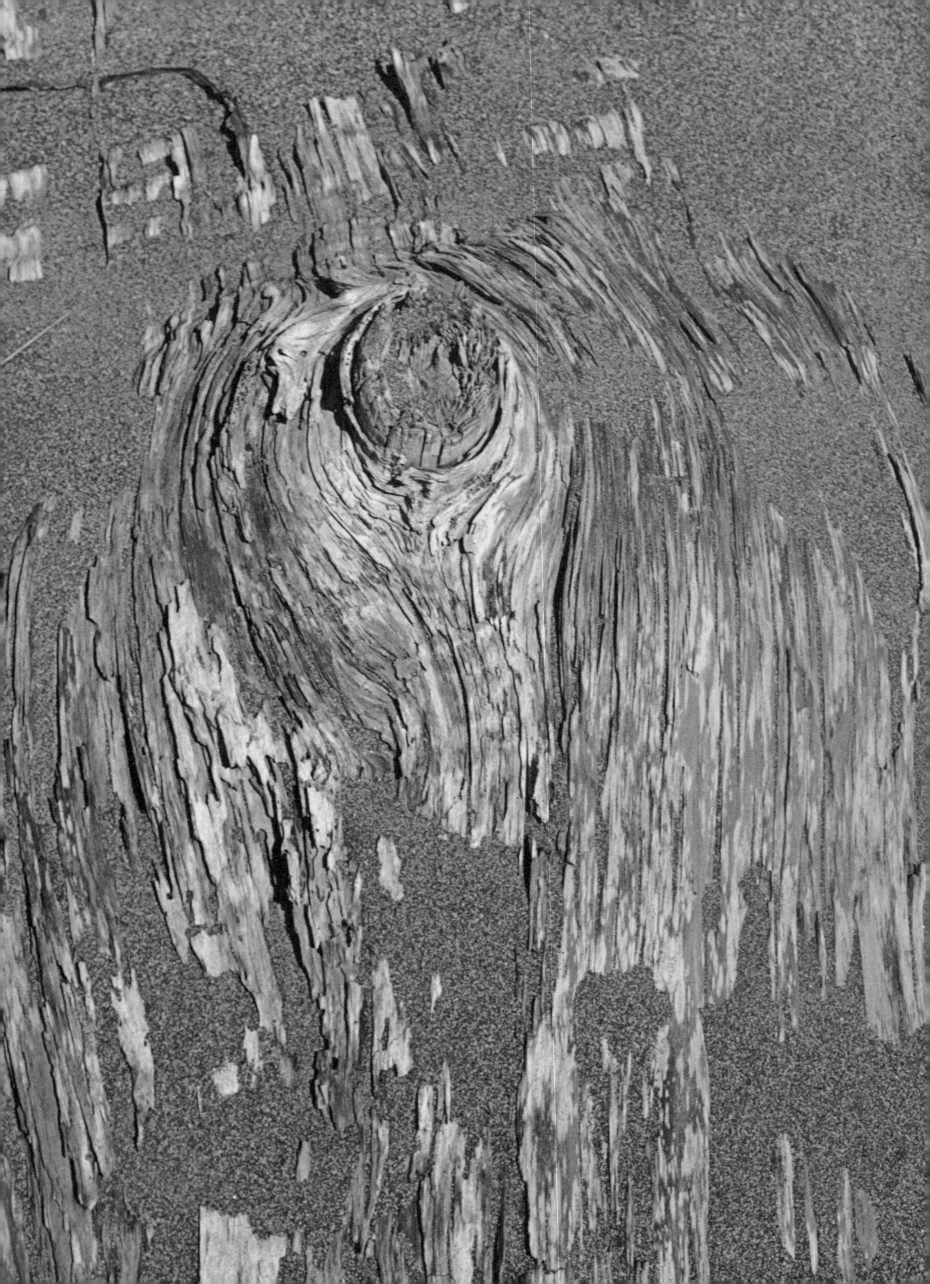

Surf at San Onofre Beach.

Surf at Table Rock.

Poinsettia, prickly pear, century plant, bougainvillea at Mission San Luis Rey. □ Fisherman on Table Rock, Aliso Beach.

Herring gull, Coronado.

Mission San Diego.

Torrey Pines State Reserve.

Egrets at Solana Beach.

Stairway to South Carlsbad Beach.

Aliso Beach, south of Laguna Beach.

White pigeons, Mission San Juan Capistrano.

Surfers, San Onofre Beach.

Ship and surfer, Huntington Beach.

Breakers under pier, Manhattan Beach.

Sand dunes at Pismo Beach.

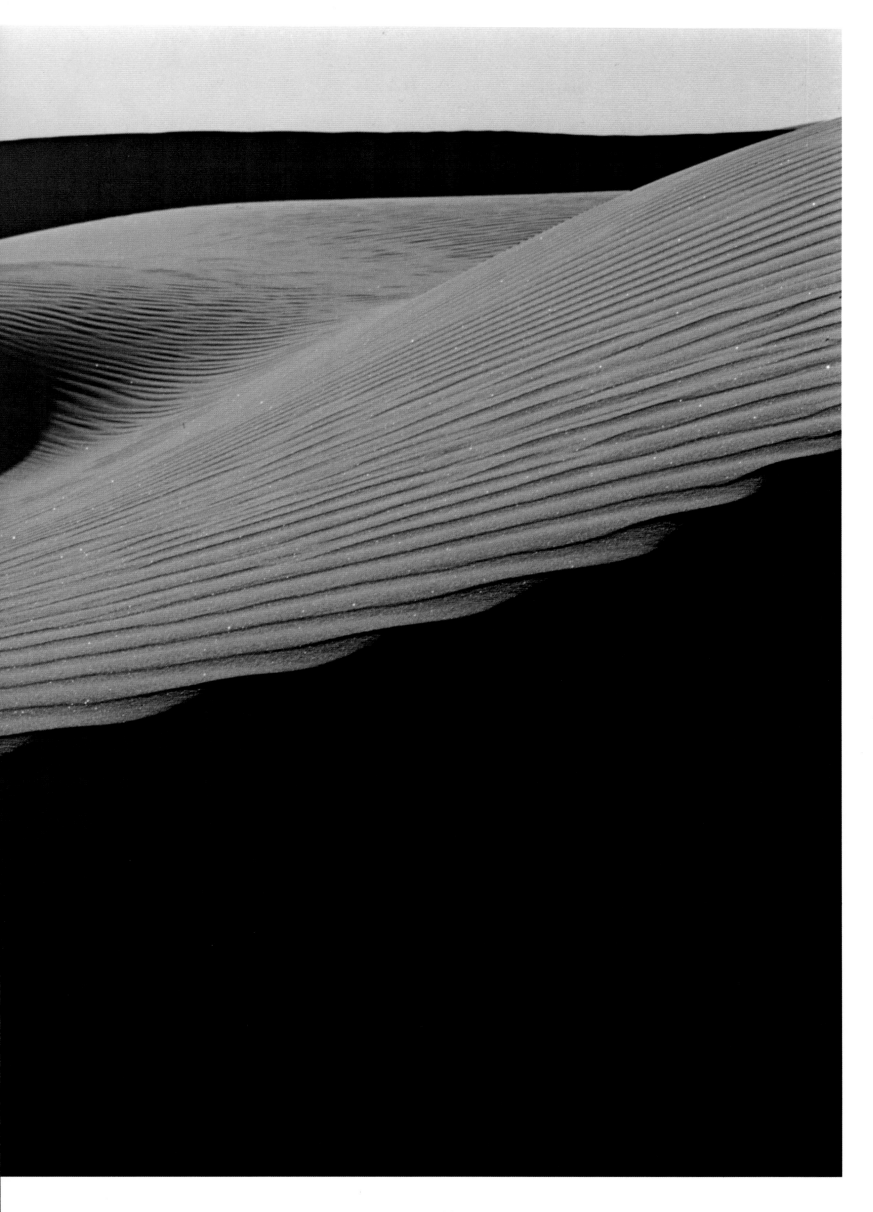

Wave at Cabrillo Point, San Pedro.

Santa Monica Mountains.

Marine life, Santa Barbara pier.

Sailboat, Marina Del Rey.

Sand patterns Pismo Beach State Park.

El Capitan Beach near Santa Barbara.

Rock formations, Santa Ynez Range.

Yucca, Santa Ynez Range.

Field mustard north of Lompoc.

Poppies and sage at Montana de Oro.

Sunset on San Simeon Beach.

Sea fig, Morro Bay.

Morro Rock across Morro Bay.

Driftwood, San Simeon State Park.

Surf at Gorda.

California poppy.

Cormorants on coast rock, near Cape San Martin. ☐ California poppy, near San Luis Obispo.

Shoreline at Bixby Creek, Big Sur.

Hillside ground cover, pine needles, thistle, Big Sur pine cones.

Coastline at Willow Creek, Big Sur. □ Walkers, Big Sur coast.

Pines in Monterey fog. □ Water textures at Pebble Beach.

Sea gulls at Point Lobos.

Carmel Mission.

Moorage lines, Fisherman's Wharf, Monterey.

62

Shoreline and marine life, Point Lobos.

Rock formations and lichen, Point Lobos.

Tide pool drain-off, Point Lobos.

Surfer, Santa Cruz.

Gooseneck barnacles and limpets, Santa Cruz. □ Natural Bridges State Park, Santa Cruz.

Beach cliff rock, Pacific Grove. □ Sea otter off Cypress Point.

Sailboats in San Francisco Bay. □ Sailboat rigging, Sausalito.

Fence and grass, Bolinas.

Surf and cliffs on McClures Beach, Point Reyes.

Poppy field near Tomales Bay.

Redwood sorrel, Muir Woods National Monument.

Eucalyptus grove near Tomales.

Beach rock on Drakes Beach, Point Reyes.

Panorama, Point Reyes National Seashore.

Sunset at Sea Ranch.

Foam and beach pebbles on the Sonoma Coast. □ Fog bank off Salt Point, Sonoma County.

Fog-covered grass, Fort Ross.

Mendocino Coast near Point Arena.

Field mustard on the Mendocino Coast.

Storm clouds over Mendocino Coast.

Mendocino Coast north of Elk.

Fog near Sea Ranch.

Coastal barn and fence near Rockport.

Beach from Patrick's Point.

Redwood National Park.

Surf and sand, Humboldt County.

Mouth of the Smith River.

Coastal rock from Trinidad.

Eucalyptus leaves, Del Norte County.

Rock on the Middle Fork, Smith River.

Beach walkers south of Eureka.

Rock shore near Big Lagoon.

Breakers at Crescent City.

Fog-covered sea, Redwood National Park.

Driftwood on Dry Lagoon Beach.

Redwood grove west of Leggett. □ Beach rock on Dry Lagoon Beach.

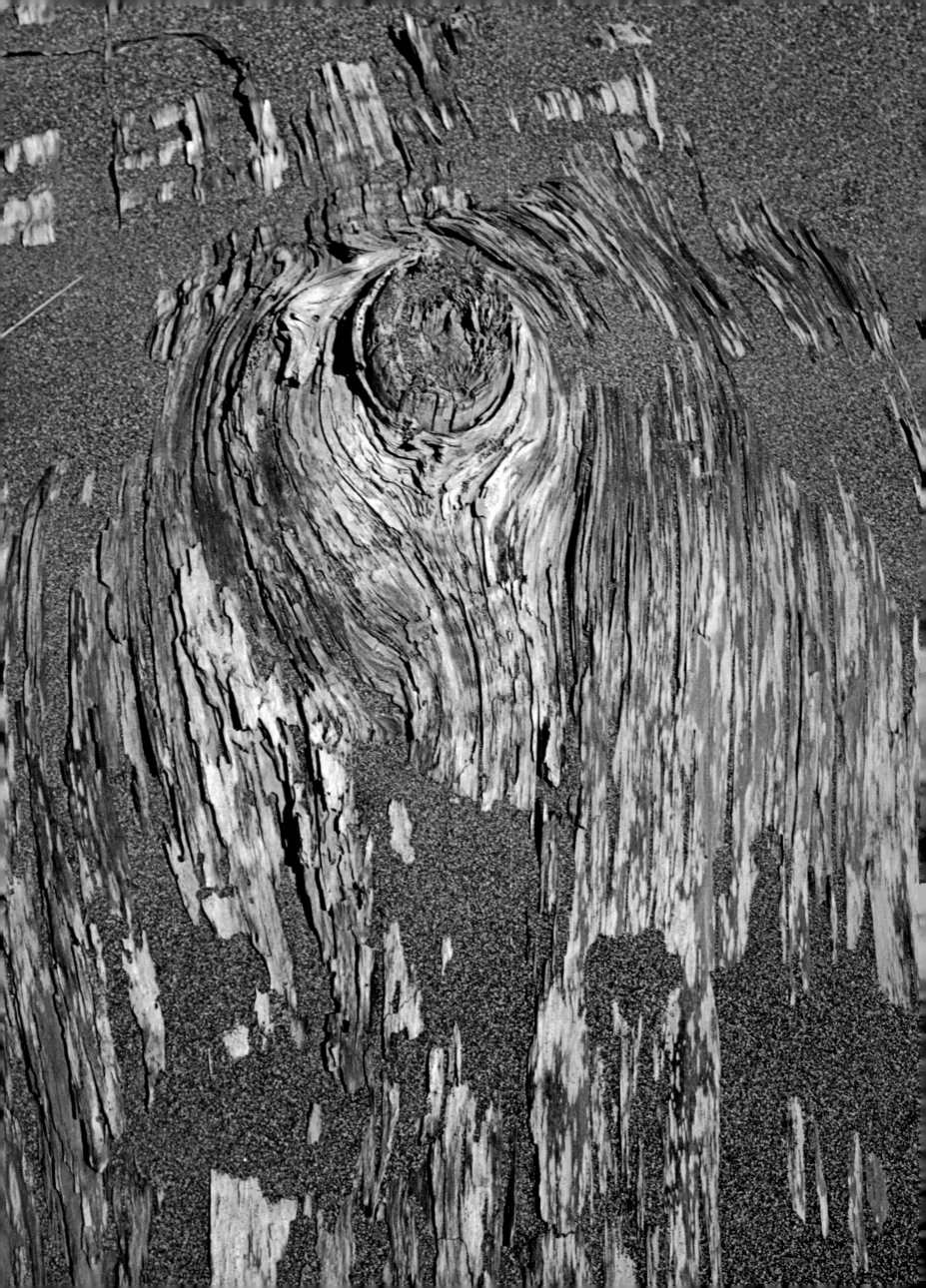

Driftwood and sand, Little River. ☐ Middle Fork, Smith River.

Sunset near the mouth of Smith River.

Fog over the Del Norte redwoods.

Sand and root mounds in Anza-Borrego Desert State Park.

THE DESERT

TEXT BY RUTH KIRK

It was spring and we were camped at Anza-Borrego, just over the mountains from San Diego. The day had begun with a sudden flaming of salmon pink reflected on the undersides of buttermilk clouds. Then the sun itself cleared the crags east of us and shone in our eyes, rimming our lashes with fire and turning our noses a glowing orange.

Dawn on the desert is time to forsake sleeping bags in favor of a walk, and this particular morning we set out down the wash nearest our camp. Paloverde trees were in blossom, touching the banks with occasional bursts of chrome yellow, and sand verbena and correopsis added splashes of purple and more yellow. Brilliant red flowers tipped each whiplike branch of ocotillo bushes and we noticed the green of new leaves, indication of recent rain. Ocotillo is so superbly adapted to the desert that it functions without leaves most of the time, letting its thorny stems carry on minimal physiological processes. Then when rain falls, soft green leaves an inch long suddenly upholster the whole plant and ocotillo catch up on food production and build reserves against the next drought, which of course is sure to come.

Two male orioles were feeding in the ocotillos that morning—a Scott's oriole, yellow with a black hood, and a Bullock's oriole, orange with a black back plus a black eye stripe and chin stripe. The Scott's was hopping from one flower head to the next, making the limber branches sway wildly. From time to time he would pause to pour out song as melodious as that of a meadowlark and while feeding he kept up a *twit-twit* call.

The Bullock's oriole feasted more deliberately and slowly, and was utterly silent. He finished with the flowers of one branch tip, then stretched his neck and caught the end of a blossom on an adjoining stem as it blew past. Drawing it close with his bill, he reached out and grabbed it with one foot. This let him resume feeding, probing delicately into each flowerlet, extracting pollen and insects and probably sipping nectar as well. The only problem was that the wind kept the two branches bobbing out of sync with each other. Straddling them was awkward, and at length the oriole stepped across the chasm to feed in peace.

We walked on. The sun was beginning to warm the wash, and battalions of harvester ants were climbing from their nests and streaming across the coarse gravel. In minutes there were two lines, one heading out, the other returning with yellow paloverde petals waving aloft like heraldic banners. The plant material would be used as mulch for the fungus gardens these ants cultivate deep within their chambers. The fungi in turn would feed the colony.

In the paloverde tree itself we could hear bees buzzing and a verdin was perched quietly, looking like a yellow-and-orange cotton Easter chick from Japan somehow come to life. Ahead, a lizard scampered to safety and a roundtail squirrel dropped into its hole, disturbed by our approach.

The morning was an ordinary one, the wash nondescript, the burgeoning of life typical. Yet we were in the heart of the supposedly bleak desert, a dry, calico land of grays and browns. Such terrain is nature's lost cause in the opinion of many—but those who think so must never have gone for a dawn walk.

Or perhaps I am unable to see desert as it is stereotyped. Among my earliest memories are nights spent beneath desert stars and later, with my ranger husband and two small sons, I lived for three years in Death Valley. A person new to desert country will stand at Hell's Gate, where the Funeral Mountains drop down to Death Valley, and staring into the great sink spread below will see only vast emptiness and desolation. Salt flats stretch for 200 square miles completely sterile. Summer temperatures climb into the 130°s Fahrenheit. Rain may start to trail from the gray underbelly of a cloud but it usually evaporates before it can wet desert soil.

This is Death Valley, yet even twenty years after living there I can't start down that slope without a flooding sense of homecoming. I know that the notch of one canyon cutting the skyline ahead holds a running stream shaded by cottonwood trees, and that there is a hillside green with watercress in another canyon. One of the dusty roads that looks as if it goes straight to nowhere, I know leads to a talc mine and I keep remembering the cookhouse with coffee and apple pie and talk at all hours, and the huge fig tree and the spring with a pool big enough to swim in hollowed from the rock.

It was mid April when we arrived in Death Valley to live. Carrying boxes into the plywood shanty that had become ours, I noticed a thermometer tacked to a mesquite by the door. It stood at 106° F., and nearly every day from then until October, when it rained, the mercury continued to climb to 100° or higher. Twenty days in May were over 100°, all of June, July, and August, twenty-two days in September, and ten in October.

The wood of our chairs shrank enough that the mortises came unglued and the screws fell out. The pages of books turned brittle. Salts clogged the head of the shower and the way to bathe was to first ream out the holes with a pin. Static electricity held dirt in our Navajo rugs with a vicelike grip, and it shot blue sparks from the sheets every time we turned over at night. Touching the kitchen faucet gave a shock. So did kissing.

Yet it was peaceful. Nobody washed windows or waxed floors or kept the cookie jar full. A woman's only household worry was that wind gusting under the door might blow out the flame of the butane refrigerator and melt the ice cubes. Shade was to sit in. Time was for going patrolling with your ranger husband, or watching the clouds gather along the mountaintops. You would notice the lizards running on tiptoe from the shade of one bush to the next, holding their tails arched up over their backs, and you'd laugh not because they looked odd but because you knew how they felt. You waited for shadows to finger across the valley at day's end bringing the cooling balm of sundown, and when they came you savored them.

Summertime in Death Valley means living in the hottest place on earth (and, in the 1950s, when we were there the houses were without air conditioning). Aziza, Libya claims a record of 136° F. against Death Valley's all-time high of 134° F., but meteorologists question the Libyan reading because nearby stations reported much lower maximums that particular day. In any case, July maximums in Death Valley consistently average higher than anywhere else in the world—and this is true even though Weather Bureau readings are taken at Furnace Creek which is higher in elevation than Badwater, the ultimate, below-sea-level sink of the valley and the spot with the highest maximums. The official July mean maximums for Death Valley typically range between 115° and 120°, and there may easily be need to drink a quart of water an hour, not just to slake uncomfortable thirst but to maintain necessary hydration.

On the other hand, there is another side to the desert's temperature story: cold. Not severe enough cold to make liars out of desert chambers of commerce, but sufficient to be a very real factor in desert habitat. Saguaro cactus, the tall candelabra-like species that symbolizes the American desert, barely crosses the Colorado River into California from Arizona. California soil is suitable but the winters are too cold. Among birds in the Mojave (and the rest of the Southwest desert) there is one that hibernates for the winter, like a bear curled into its den in the northern pine forest. This is the poorwill, a squat nocturnal bird that ordinarily snatches insects on the wing by making abrupt little leaps from the ground.

Poorwills feed efficiently at dawn and dusk, cramming their stomachs, handling large grasshoppers by folding them double as they swallow. When winter comes such insect feasts become difficult and rather than fight the cold without adequate body fuel, the poorwill simply opts out. It selects a rocky crevice and settles in. Internal temperature plummets from a normal of 106° F. to 64.4° and becomes comparable to a man letting his system cool from 98.6° to about 68°. Even with a stethoscope, no heartbeat can be picked up and breathing is so slight that the chest doesn't seem to move. A mirror held to the nasal openings show no condensation.

Hibernation takes only about one-tenth the energy needed for simple resting, and it saves drastically more compared with normal activity. By using one gram of body fat every ten days a poorwill can easily make it through the winter.

Actually it wasn't until a few decades ago that science learned about the desert's "sleeping bird." Southwest Indian people and desert prospectors knew, but the idea of hibernating birds had become almost a symbol of biological misconceptions to most informed people. The notion once had been used to explain the disappearance and re-emergence of swallows; then migration came to be recognized and fairly well understood and hibernation among birds was laughed off. But in 1946 Dr. Edmund Jaeger, dean of California desert naturalists, decided to investigate.

That winter he found a poorwill crouched motionless in a rock crevice. He touched it, he shouted, he picked it up, and the bird made no response except to open one eyelid, its only sign of life. Ten days later Jaeger returned and the poorwill was still crouched in the little cleft, still "sleeping." This time, however, it flew after repeated handling.

The frosty cold of the desert that prompts the bird's hibernation has somehow escaped widespread attention although it was discovered by the first party to enter California overland. This was a band of 240 persons, mostly women and children, accompanied by Spanish soldiers and some 800 head of cattle, horses, and sheep. They were en route from Mexico to San Francisco where they were to reinforce the presidio, for this was the late 18th Century when New Spain stretched northward to an indeterminate limit, and forts flying the Spanish colors dotted the coast as far north as Nootka, British Columbia.

Lieutenant Colonel Juan Bautista de Anza led the *entrada*. Two years earlier he had pioneered the route, heading an expedition at his own expense to prove its feasibility. At the time Spaniards spoke of "California" when they meant what today is called Baja California, and of "Alta California" when they referred to the northern portion, which was considered something of an appendage. In the Mexico of that day, Baja California was easily reached by a short voyage from the mainland and it was relatively well settled. To the north, Alta California formed a little-known frontier held by a string of missions and a few presidios. The journey to reach it was arduous. Vessels had to beat their way from San Blas against unfavorable winds and tides, and to travel northward from the Gulf settlements by land was infinitely worse than the voyage by sea because of rugged mountains and desolate stretches of desert.

All of California was believed to be an island at that time, despite occasional reports to the contrary. In 1702 Father Eusebio Francisco Kino, the indomitable Jesuit of Sonora and Arizona, had confirmed earlier rumors that Upper California could be reached overland and that Lower California was a peninsula. But his report had languished and been forgotten.

Nonetheless the possibility that the missions from San Diego to San Francisco could be supplied by land via Sonora and Arizona was revived in de Anza's mind when he heard Sonoran Indians gossiping about what the Spanish were doing in Alta California. If such news could spread so rapidly from tribe to tribe, he reasoned, there must be a land connection westward from the Colorado River.

Father Francisco Hermenegildo Garcés, missionary at Tucson's San Javier del Bac, had traveled as far as the Colorado River delta in 1771 and his reports further fueled de Anza's determination to establish a supply route. Proving such an approach feasible was important, for the Spanish crown was feeling a new need to safeguard its ill-defined northern claims. Russian traders were beginning to work southward from Alaska, and the sails of English mariners were occasionally appearing as well.

De Anza made a pioneering trek across what now is Arizona and entered Imperial County, California, in 1774. He reported on this expedition, accepted promotion and praise for it, and then after mass on September 29 of the following year, he again set out from Tubac, Arizona. This time he was leading colonists and soldiers.

By early December this second expedition had crossed the Colorado and swung south to avoid the vast sand dunes west of Yuma. De Anza now divided the party into three groups which were to travel one day apart to avoid exhausting pasturage and

water through this bleak section. Thus prepared for the expected extreme of the desert, they were met instead by a snowstorm and biting cold. Six head of cattle, one mule, and ten horses perished and frostbite was rampant among all personnel. One man was so severely affected that "it was necessary to bundle him up for two hours between four fires" in order to save his life, according to the official account of this initial encounter with the California desert.

Even so, the three units at length were reunited, the weather warmed, and the occasion was celebrated with a fandango at a spot known today as Harper's Well, a few miles southwest of the Salton Sea. Two weeks later, on January 4, 1776, the weary party arrived at the San Gabriel Mission and, after resting, started on for San Francisco. The desert had been successfully crossed and Alta California was linked with certainty to the continent.

Unexpected cold is not the only underplayed attribute of desert country. There is also unexpected moisture. Consider Death Valley as an example. Rainfall there scarcely amounts to an inch-and-one-half per year (and for the California desert as a whole it ranges from three or four inches to a scant ten inches per year). Yet dry as the land is, marshes and ponds are not uncommon. Frederick Colville, a pioneering botanist, listed forty-eight species of marsh plants in Death Valley and an equal number needing moist soil. At the time we lived in the Valley the reservoir kept for fire protection of the headquarters buildings doubled as a swimming pool, and it was not uncommon to find coots and teal paddling there when we arrived to swim.

Snipes, killdeers, and ducks were common along Salt Creek and Saratoga Springs, in the middle of the supposedly dry valley floor, and even a cursory check of coyote scat showed that waterfowl were abundant enough to be a dependable food source. Snowy egrets occasionally came to the irrigation ditches at Furnace Creek Ranch where alfalfa and dates were raised, and in fall and spring we sometimes heard the wild honking of migrating geese. Once in a while a flock traveling at night would mistake the white shimmer of Death Valley's salt flats for open water and settle to rest. Often they were too exhausted to take off again, and died.

Death Valley's aquatic life even includes fish, inch-long members of the *Cyprinidae* family, commonly called pupfish. We used to swim with them at Saratoga Springs and Big Hole—deep pools of crystal water that dot the sterile immensity of the land, typical of isolated springs and marshes throughout the desert. During the last ice age the fish belonged to a vast system of waterways that flooded what now are dry valleys and formed deep lakes, which often were interconnected by spillways and rivers. For millennia they swam undisturbed, then ten or twelve thousand years ago the climate warmed and the waters all but vanished. That might well have been the end of the pupfish except for one characteristic: adaptability.

With a mutation rate that excites geneticists, small, widely separated populations managed to adjust to various new realities. Today pupfish tolerate temperature fluctuations from near simmering in summer to almost freezing in winter, and they endure salt concentrations greater than that of the ocean. They may live in as little as an inch or two of water and if it evaporates a few will survive in whatever bottom ooze remains.

Such adaptation is remarkable because fish, and all forms of aquatic life, ordinarily experience an environment that stays at a constant temperature. Yet somehow, when the need arose, pupfish were able to change. They survived the radical shifts in environment. They have withstood pressure from the feeding of ducks and herons and predacious beetles, and from desert Indians who used to scoop them up with baskets. But the little fish may now be meeting their end as a species. Modern man's desert agriculture is altering water tables and drying the habitat of some pupfish populations, and non-native fishes that have been introduced into their home waters in several places also pose a threat.

Throughout the desert, native fishes are endangered. Fish are the most numerous of the world's invertebrates, both in species and in total numbers. There are some 20,000 different kinds in the oceans and fresh waters of the earth, and a total of more than 1,000 in the lakes and rivers of the United States alone, nearly all of them in the East. The dry lands of the American Southwest harbor no more than fifty species and most of these are in jeopardy. Many survive in pools scarcely bigger than bathtubs. The entire population of their kind may number no more than twenty or thirty. Yet they remain, relics of the past that refuse to die; living fossils.

The springs and streams of the desert are pinpoints of moisture on the overall dryness of the land. Great expanses may go more than a year at a time with no rain, supporting only sparse life and bouncing the sun's rays back from a parched and stony surface. Even so, it is water that shapes the landscape, for when a storm does come, as little as a fraction of an inch of rain can have a drastic effect.

Runoff is prodigious, and as trickles drain from enormous catchment basins they flood into narrow canyons as raging torrents. Once when returning from the grocery store—which was 100 miles from our house—we were delayed for two hours while a brown stream thirty feet wide rampaged across the road. Yet not a drop of rain had fallen in the miles we had traveled. Such occurrences are not rare, and they usually are much more severe. A wait of two days—or two weeks—is as likely as a mere two hours. Roads can be washed out or covered with debris that includes large rocks. A single two-hour storm in the White Mountains east of Bishop a few years ago sent water and mud forty to sixty feet deep sluicing into the narrows of a canyon. At the mouth, the flood fanned out and flowed as a slurry mix about two feet deep, veneering the desert floor

The process, perhaps during an earlier, wetter period, built the great alluvial fans that spill from the mountain canyons and lie as rocky aprons against desert ranges. Water is thus the sculptor of the Southwest as surely as of the Northwest or the Appalachians, even though few rivers run openly across the land. Those that do usually are born of mountain snows far beyond the desert itself.

However, the seemingly dry courses of rivers usually are moist deep within their gravel. Because of this, trees such as paloverde, smoke tree, mesquite, and ironwood follow the drainage channels of the desert. They are able to send their roots deep. Fifty to 100 feet is common for mesquite roots, and the scientific literature mentions one case of mesquite penetrating 175 feet to reach water.

Smoke tree and paloverde grow most readily along washes, not only because of their roots, but also because their seeds are encased in hard coatings that must be cracked before germination can begin. This happens only in the churning wake of a cloudburst, and the process both opens the seed coats and assures sprouting seedlings the moisture they need for survival. Roots push out quickly to tap this moisture. A smoke tree barely an inch high may have roots more than two feet long.

Other plants follow an opposite pattern. Instead of sinking roots deep to find water they spread them out barely beneath the soil surface. These plants are opportunists waiting for the least sprinkle to trail from a passing cloud. A few species even send out what are known as "rain roots," hairlike structures that lengthen rapidly so long as the moisture lasts, then wither and fall off. Some bushes sheath their roots with mucus that picks up sand and forms a sort of earthen pipe to protect against drying. Others develop a corky covering with a spongy water storage layer just inside it to supply moisture for the active root tissue.

In several species of plants, stems carry on photosynthesis in the place of leaves. Cactus are the best known example, but walking the desert you also notice bushes that are adapted in this way. Desert tea and desert rue are perhaps the most widespread of such bushes. They look like low tangles of leafless green twigs, although examination will reveal vestigial leaves little bigger than scales.

Bushes with leaves typically have small ones. The less surface there is, the less the risk of losing excessive moisture through transpiration. Someone has calculated that the leaf surface of an acre of Mojave Desert plants scarcely equals that of a single surburban maple tree. Leaves may be reduced to mere scales, or they may be borne and dropped as conditions dictate, as in the case of ocotillo

One time soon after we had moved to the desert I walked across a hillside deliberately noticing the leaves of the scraggly bushes that dotted the rocky slope. Almost all were thick, presenting a high ratio of mass to surface. Many were wax-coated; others were matted with hairs to reflect heat and help to hold in moisture. A few species of plants—although none I saw that particular day—actually fold their leaves at midday to hide pores from the sun. Others turn edgewise and thereby minimize exposure.

Creosote bush, the lacey bush that is the most widespread of all the plants of the American Desert, has three distinct types of leaves. These are shed successively as drought settles in until only the small, hard little leaves of the third type remain. They are the most drought resistant leaves known in the world. A loss of cell moisture as great as eighty per cent of normal doesn't deter minimal functioning for these leaves.

Plants that meet desert conditions in this way are termed drought evaders. They escape reality by closing up shop and waiting for better times. Others are called drought resisters. They absorb water greedily while it is available and horde it within their tissue as internal reservoirs to be drawn upon as needed. Cacti follow this method. Visitors to the desert find them blooming and setting fruit even in years when no rain has fallen and other flowers are scarce. Cacti are capable of living for months at a time completely independent of external moisture conditions. Desert animals from cactus mice to jackrabbits and javelinas know this source of moisture and feed on cactus as unperturbed by thorns as if they were munching cucumbers. Men, too, have relied on the lifesaving moisture of cactus, particularly that of barrel cactus, named for its size and shape. Legend holds that these plants are living tanks of water, which of course is untrue. They are filled inside with a moist pulp not unlike that of watermelon—although totally lacking the sweetness and pleasant taste of melon.

Every few years a precise combination of rainfall and temperature occur in November and December, resulting months later in a spectacular corsage of spring blossoms. Drive through the desert at these times and you find entire hillsides painted with the yellows and reds and purples and whites of desert sunflower, poppy, penstemon, mallow, verbena, lupine, primrose, and a host of others. Such periods of flowering touch the drab and stony land as a miracle. Yet to stop with simply marveling is to miss the greatest beauty of all, for the desert operates on a plan as surely as does the seashore or the forest.

A great deal of study has gone into deciphering the plan, and much remains to be done. As one botanist has commented: "The explanation is bound to be as complex as the phenomena it seeks to clarify." Studies that seem to establish certain rules governing the sprouting and flowering of desert annuals have to be questioned as additional studies are completed, and what holds true for one species or set of conditions may only mislead when applied to other species or conditions. Even so, certain patterns have become plain.

The showpieces of the desert flora are the ephemerals, the annuals that neither resist nor evade drought but escape it altogether. These are the species that transform the desert into patchwork gardens. They grow whenever and wherever soil, moisture, and temperature permit, and between times they wait out unfavorable conditions in dormancy, as seeds. If need be, they wait for years. Too much rain or too little, or the wrong timing in relation to temperature, and they hold over as seeds instead of sprouting. But let there be about a half inch of rain in November coupled with temperatures in the 50°s and 60°s F. and a flower show is certain by February.

Two types of enzymes control whether seeds will germinate or remain dormant. One type is a growth inhibitor, the other a growth stimulator. Rainfall in just the right amount leaches out the one and activates the other. Moisture that is too scant to assure growth is also too scant to rid seeds of their inhibitor enzymes, and whatever inhibitors are washed out by a skimpy rain tend to rebuild. Consequently the next shower has the whole job to do and the odds start anew.

Rain that falls too quickly also accomplishes nothing. The inhibitors of some species diffuse slowly. In others an excessively hard rain leaches out growth stimulators right along with the inhibitors and thereby sets the whole process back to the beginning, like returning to "Start" on a Parcheesi board after you've made it halfway around.

To the human mind desert conditions seem unfavorable for plants, but the feeling is born of our familiarity with the controlled moisture and fertility of farms and city gardens. Hundreds of plants are thoroughly at home in the desert—600 species in Death Valley alone—and many couldn't live under what to us would seem more desirable circumstances.

The oldest living things in the world, so far as known, belong to the desert. They are the bristlecone pines of the high ridges that tower thousands of feet above the sere lowlands. Go to the Panamint Mountains edging Death Valley on the west to see them, or to the White Mountains northwest of there. Roads lead to the high slopes where the trees grow—elevations of 7000 to 11,000 feet—and to see the patriarchs you follow well marked trails. Limber pines intermix with the bristlecones. Their needles come in short tufts at the ends of the branches, fairly easy to distinguish from bristlecones, which have needles running back along the branch tips for a foot or more.

Where growing conditions provide ample moisture and shelter, bristlecones may grow eighty feet high and as straight and symmetrical as a woodlot pine. But these favored trees are not the ones that attain great age. The ancient specimens belong to the wind-blasted crags and ridges. They are so gnarled and twisted that they look like Japanese bonsai on a mistaken, large scale. Growth rings are set so close together that it takes a microscope to count them. A full century may add only an inch to the diameter of these trees, and one six feet high may be 500 years old. Twenty-five to thirty feet high is about maximum for the truly old bristlecones, whose ages are counted in thousands of years. One bristlecone in the White Mountains has been cored and found 4,600 years old; others nearby are over 4,000 years. A bristlecone pine in the Snake Mountains of Nevada was 4,900 years old, but someone cut it down to use in a dating study—an unforgivable travesty.

The extreme age of the bristlecones has only been known for twenty years, which is no time at all in the life of trees that were already aged when Moses received the Ten Commandments and when the pyramids began to rise above the sands of Egypt. In 1948 United States Forest Service men sectioned pines in the White Mountains and found them 900 years old, impressive but scarcely in league with the sequoias which were believed the world's oldest living species. Then in 1956 Dr. Edmund Schulman of the University of Arizona found a living White Mountain bristlecone with 4,000 annual rings.

Schulman's specialty was geochronology based on tree rings, a system developed at the University of Arizona to date archaeological ruins and other remnants of the past. Seeking to push the dating farther back in time, Schulman had made a survey of ancient trees wherever he could find them. He cored an 860-year-old ponderosa in Bryce National Park, Utah, and a 975-year-old pinyon pine several miles north of the park. Near Sun Valley, Idaho, he had found a limber pine 1,400 years old. And then he heard of the White Mountain bristlecones and decided to test them.

In time he identified several that are over 4,000 years old and therefore older than sequoias by about a thousand years. The first of the ancient bristlecones is called Pine Alpha and it has become a point of pilgrimage, reached by a half-mile path beyond the White Mountain picnic area at an elevation of 10,600 feet.

The trunk of this tree measures four feet thick with its total living bark a strip that is no more than ten inches wide. This seems to be the secret of the bristlecones' longevity. They don't fight the odds by trying to keep all of their cells alive. Instead,

they largely die back and leave alive only the portion of their great bulk that conditions actually permit them to support. A battered and aged tree such as Pine Alpha still produces viable seed, still contributes to the genetic pool of the oncoming generations.

Plant life determines animal life in the desert, as elsewhere, for animal tissue is reconstituted plant tissue, whether that of a scorpion or a kangaroo rat, a mountain lion or a human being. Sometimes a plant-animal relationship works both ways, each life-form linked to the other for survival. A classic case is the interdependence of yuccas and *Pronuba* moths. The yuccas are oversize members of the lily family which range as much as twenty or thirty feet tall in the case of Joshua trees. All species bear fibrous, swordlike blades that make the plants look like living pincushions, and the flowers of all species form spikes of creamy blossoms.

The moths come to the flowers not to feed but to lay their eggs, and in the process they pollinate the yuccas. No place except the green fruit of the plants will do for the eggs because the hatching caterpillars depend on the developing seeds for their food supply; and no means other than the moths' visit could possibly pollinate the yuccas and assure their perpetuation.

More than a mere depositing of eggs takes place. Some added urge prompts the females to gather balls of pollen and ram them down the pistils of the flowers. They don't feed on this pollen; neither do their offspring. Nonetheless, they pack it carefully into the tube of the pistil, pushing it down hard. Their diligence is essential, for the pistils of yucca are so constricted toward the base that wind pollination would be impossible. Only the moths' deliberate ramming can do the job. If it weren't for this care from the moths, there would be no yuccas. And if it weren't for the yuccas, there would be no *Pronuba* moths.

For Joshua trees this particular interrelationship is only one of many. A species of lizard known as a night lizard lives its entire life in the shaggy bark and decay cavities of fallen Joshuas, feeding on grubs, ants, and termites, and never venturing beyond this tightly bounded realm. Two dozen or more bird species favor Joshua trees as nesting sites, including red-shafted flickers which hollow out holes that are later occupied by Baird wrens, plain titmice, Western bluebirds, ash-throated flycatchers, and screech owls.

Desert Indians also counted on Joshua trees, and other yuccas. A frothy liquid made from the roots could be swallowed as a laxative or used as a shampoo. Leaves provided fiber for sandals and for nets used to snare rabbits. Flower heads could be cut while still in bud and roasted in fire pits as a spring delicacy.

The dependence of animal life on plants is well known and usually the relationship is fairly simple and direct. In contrast, consider the interaction between mesquite trees, the mistletoe that parasitizes them, and the birds that come to eat the mistletoe berries.

Bluebirds, mockingbirds, Gila woodpeckers, and robins all feed in the dense clusters of mistletoe infecting the trees, and Gambel's quail pick up the berries that fall to the ground. Most of all, phainopeplas, or silky flycatchers, are the birds associated with desert mistletoe. In the dry outskirts of Palm Springs, I remember once watching one of these glossy black birds gobble twelve watery berries without so much as a change of position. Then he hopped to a new toehold and gulped down twenty-three more. Next he flew to the topmost branch of the tree and from there sallied out after insects, feeding on the wing. The perch evidently was a favorite, for a mound of droppings the size of a football had caught in the branches directly beneath.

Most of this bulk was undigested mistletoe seeds—and herein lies a controversy. Some ecologists call phainopeplas the worst waster in the desert, for none of the seeds in these masses can germinate and produce new mistletoe plants. The bird's habit is against its own self-interest, according to this reasoning, for the mistletoe is a valuable food resource.

Other ecologists argue just the opposite. If a substantially greater proportion of mistletoe did manage to establish itself, they point out, the only possible long-range effect would be more of the parasite than mesquites could withstand. Mistletoe would eliminate its host, and thereby bring on its own doom. The phainopepla intervenes constructively, according to this line of reasoning. By devouring seeds and depositing them in such a way as to prevent their sprouting, the birds aid the longevity of mesquite. That assures a future for the parasite, and its continuance promises berries for phainopeplas and a score of other desert creatures. Balance is maintained.

Few desert seeds come packaged in watery pulp, as is true of mistletoe, yet seeds may provide the only moisture source for desert creatures such as the kangaroo rat. These are silky-furred rodents named for their long hind legs and short fore-legs—immensely appealing little animals leaping at the edge of a campfire's gleam or, occassionally, encountered in the day-time.

The desert world as these rodents experience it differs from what we humans experience. Our official temperature readings are taken from thermometers housed in louvred boxes set a standard five feet above the ground, and this realm has no meaning for kangaroo rats. The temperature of the ground surface where they scamper sometimes soars as high as 190° F. at mid-day, far above Weather Bureau maximums. To escape this heat, kangaroo rats spend the daytime in their burrows where temperatures remain twenty or thirty per cent lower than air temperatures outside and about half of what the soil surface is capable of registering.

Such systems of beating the heat are common. Badgers, kit foxes, and coyotes all burrow underground. Ringtail cats seek the shelter of an old mine tunnel or a rock crevice. Rattlesnakes wriggle beneath the protection of a rock or sometimes glide into a rodent burrow, hunting a cool retreat more than a meal.

For animals as small as kangaroo rats (four or five inches long depending on species) avoiding heat is extremely important, yet the habit is not enough to serve as their only desert adaptation. Physiologists have found that these animals never drink water even when kept in rooms that were heated to simulate desert conditions. Obviously they were getting water somewhere; all life depends on it. But the source was not by drinking. Dishes of water in the cages were never touched. Neither were the laboratory kangaroo rats eating succulent food.

The only possible source of moisture seemed to be metabolic water—and this proved the answer. All animals manufacture this water as food is metabolized, or digested, but the amount is so small it is inconsequential for most species. However, for kangaroo rats it is the total supply. They manage this chiefly through the efficiency of their kidneys. Body wastes are so concentrated that they require very little water for elimination—so little that metabolic water alone suffices to keep tissues moist and functioning and also to take care of excretion.

Perhaps the only system that could be more finely tuned to desert realities would be to also have an internal water reservoir. A camel's hump often is thought to be a water supply, although it actually is an energy reserve of fat, not of moisture. It is amphibians and reptiles that have internal "canteens."

Spadefoot toads are an example. They burst from the desert sands during summer rainstorms to congregate at puddles and perpetuate their kind. About ten months of the year they spend dormant, encased in a self-made horny cocoon that covers all but their nostrils and helps prevent body dehydration. The water of their bladder carries them through this long period. Body wastes are stored as urea which can be held in chemical suspension to be excreted later, after the toad has stirred to active life again and found a rain puddle.

Chuckawallas, the largest lizards in the California desert, twelve to fifteen inches long, have a pair of sacs that run along each side from jaw to groin. These hold a special clear liquid that forms as the lizards feed on moist vegetation. During periods of drought they slowly empty. Tortoises have similar water sacs to tide them through the worst of the desert's dry periods.

The mechanisms that let these animals survive have only recently begun to be identified, and the same is true for precise knowledge of man's physiology in the desert. As short a time ago as World War II, troops readying for combat in North Africa were training in the California desert on water allowances of one gallon per man per day for all purposes, including washing. At least this was the regimen that General George Patton was seeking to impose. In actuality, it resulted in a great deal of practice for medics and an unprecedented chance for physiologists to study how the body adjusts, and fails to adjust, to the desert.

Water proved the only means a human has for adapting—quantities of water to pour out as sweat and keep the internal tissues and organs cool. Without water a man will perish. The human body is about two thirds water, by weight, and it needs to stay that way. Even so small a loss as one per cent of body moisture drastically lowers efficiency and well-being. A single day without water at a temperature of 120° F. will usually bring death. If one gallon is available and a man remains inactive he will live for two days. At least these are the rules of thumb.

Actually, attitude and good sense make a great deal of difference. A man who is panicked may die with water still in his canteen. On the other hand, one who exerts only at night and spends the day resting quietly in the shade will raise his odds greatly. If he makes a still—or several stills— to supply himself with water his chances shoot up even more. The method is simple. All that is needed is a piece of plastic sheeting and a hole dug about one or two feet deep and three feet in diameter. Simply cover the hole with the plastic, letting it sag three or four inches above the bottom of the hole and sealing the edge tightly with sand or stone. Then place a small stone in the middle of the plastic to weight it into a cone, and beneath the center point set any available container—a jar, a hubcap, your hat. Ideally, also lay tubing from the container to the edge of the plastic sheet so that you can suck up the water that will collect. This saves dismantling the still to reach the container.

If cactus is available, cut it in pieces and put it into the hole. If not, use other vegetation, the more succulent the better. Or simply rely on the moisture within the ground. The warmth of the sun striking the plastic will draw moisture from the ground and any vegetation that has been added to the still. Droplets will condense on the underside of the plastic and run down to the weighted point. From there they will fall into the container.

In clay or slightly damp sand a yield of two or three pints of water per day can be expected and even at night some water will be produced.

Moisture beneath the surface of the ground is certain in a wash or in an area where moisture-demanding plants such as seepwillow or arrowweed are growing. Coyotes know this and in times of drought tunnel several feet to reach damp subterranean layers.

Clothes should be kept on. They insulate against the sun's fire and they slow the loss of body moisture. Contact with the ground surface should be avoided. Rest instead on any kind of platform that raises the body a foot or so above the superheated soil surface. Don't eat. Digesting food takes water that otherwise could be used for perspiration. Never swallow brackish water, urine, or other impure liquids. However, these can be used to moisten the skin and aid evaporative cooling, or they can be poured into the bottom of the still to be drawn back up in purified form.

Perhaps most important is to think through your plight at the outset and decide a course of action. This last is what saved my husband's life once in Death Valley when his patrol truck had two flat tires. It was summer and we were being transferred out of the Valley. This was Louis' last day of duty and he had gone to the remote southern end of the Valley to post a sign warning that the road would not be patrolled. His emergency gear had all been turned in, even to the drum of water he always carried. He had only a water bag and a vacuum bottle of iced tea. The temperature was 123° F. when he had the second flat. The time was not yet noon.

Louis decided to stay where he was on the chance that someone might happen by. It was Saturday and men from a nearby talc mine might head into the town of Shoshone when evening came. If this failed, he planned to start driving an hour after dusk and if he could get within a mile of a small spring he knew about, he would walk the rest of the way. If not, he would stay with the truck. By deciding ahead, while his mind was still clear, he would not have to think later. Instead, he could tell himself that the decision had already been reached. He could follow his own orders.

Luckily, he drove to about a half mile from the spring before the wheels refused to turn farther. From there he walked. The water had a dead scorpion floating in it and was scummed over, but its taste was ambrosial.

There by the little spring, at 4:00 A.M., another ranger and I found Louis. He was little concerned by the mishap, for he remembered telling me his proposed itinerary and he was confident that I, too, knew the location of the spring. Actually, it was the fifth or sixth spring that we had checked, each of them a potential haven depending on where he had been when the trouble occurred. For me, anxiety had grown harder and harder to hold in check as each spring proved deserted. The black, hostile emptiness of that night had become ominous before we at last saw the gleam of his signal fire, still thirty miles ahead down the wash.

The facts of desert thirst and techniques for coping with it have been fairly completely worked out now, and the knowledge is both interesting and somehow reassuring. Yet what of the long procession of people who simply have lived in the desert, adjusting to its demands and calling it home?

During our years in Death Valley I took basketry lessons from Indian women who lived at Furnace Creek Ranch and sitting with them in the shade of a mesquite I used to think about the gulf between their empirical knowledge of how to cope with desert heat and our newfound scientific awareness of man's physiology under such circumstances.

One of the women still lived in a wickiup, a circular roofless windbreak built of brush that was simply lashed together. Her grandfather had met the first white men to enter Death Valley, the 1849 emigrants. Before his time there stretched scores of centuries of desert-dwelling Indians who know no world other than the dry and wrinkled land east of the Sierra and west of the Colorado. The idea of the desert as deadly never would have occurred to them.

In fact the desert tribes first encountered and described by the Spanish seem to have routinely performed feats that confound modern explanations of the maximum a man can endure. Father Garcés reported that Mojave Indians told him they could withstand hunger and thirst for as long as four days. They were renowned as runners, and often were employed as messengers. Men could travel a hundred miles in a day, trotting steadily and carrying neither food nor weapons. In small bands they roamed the desert, visiting and trading.

Today Tarahumara Indians in the Sierra Madre Occidental mountains of northern Mexico run 100- to 200-mile races in from twenty-four to forty-eight hours, and small boys hold five- or six-mile races simply for an hour's amusement.

Papago Indians in southern Arizona and Seri Indians living along the Gulf of California also were able to withstand conditions that science finds killing. Women and girls had to walk every day to springs as much as five or six miles distant carrying water to their families in pottery jars. "We knew how to use water carefully," a Papago woman is quoted by anthropologist Ruth Underhill as having explained. "We have a word that means thirst-enduring, and that is what we were taught to be."

This sort of a capacity to meet the desert on its own harsh terms is beyond today's understanding. Instead we tend to come to the desert with attitudes that were born in more moist lands. We plant lawns and build swimming pools. We promote desert real estate developments by moving London Bridge from the Thames to the Colorado and by advertising the "world's highest fountain" as a desert community's "dramatic centerpiece, shooting five feet higher than the Washington Monument in the nation's capital."

We lace the desert sands with open irrigation ditches that lose prodigious quantities of water through evaporation, and we underlie fields with mile upon mile of drain tile, then flush additional water through the soil to carry off salts. We crash through stands of creosote bush and burroweed in our jeeps, and we flip horned toads and kangaroo rats out of their burrows with the tires of our dune buggies. Each Thanksgiving for the last few years motorcyclists have lined up more than a thousand strong to race cross-country over public lands from Barstow to Las Vegas, 160 miles. The habitat destroyed in such a single day can take a century to build back. If the races were scheduled for Griffith Park or Golden Gate Park everyone would know that the land couldn't stand the pressure.

In truth, neither can the desert, and increasingly people are realizing that these lands are an awesome and beautiful entity in themselves. Not every acre needs to be plowed or built upon or raced over. Great value comes from simply letting some of it be—value for us today and most assuredly for the future.

The California desert spreads across some seventeen million acres, about 25,000 square miles. It holds broad basins, salt flats, dry lakes, sand dunes, steep mountains—and peace for anyone who cares to find it. Try walking in a wash or across the voluptious curves and wind ripples of sand dunes. Go especially at dawn or at sundown, and give yourself to the vastness and the silence. Watch also for the minute—the brush marks of a hawks' wings against the sand ending the quick but futile scamper of a mouse or the successive J marks made by a sidewinder (the smallest of the rattlesnakes) as it glides with consummate grace across the desert floor.

Perhaps there will be a pack rat nest, seemingly an aimless bushel-basket pile of twigs, cactus joints, and dried seed pods but actually a well designed abode. Loose construction allows for air flow; the thick "roof" cuts off solar radiation; the moist bits of cactus and other vegetation provide evaporative cooling.

By day the desert is brown, except for the fleeting pink and mauve of sunrise and sunset. At dusk it becomes blue, then black. Other terrains are more varied in overall hue, but the desert overdoes itself even in this regard. Maybe its oneness of color preempts part of its reputation for monotony. Maybe it is that men tend to speed across the dry reaches without taking time to feel or to truly see.

Recently, after a long absence, we drove back to the desert and again made camp, this time at the mouth of a little canyon which overlooked a smoothly floored basin. On this particular return the desert impressed us with its sense of isolation from all that we dislike. Mayhem and war seem so ridiculous as to be impossible when you stand alone in this kind of space with only an unseen ribbon of asphalt to represent civilization.

To an extent, the same feeling comes at the seashore or the mountains, but in the desert you see more uncluttered square miles at a time. And the space is balm for crowded, frenetic everyday lives. Furthermore the beach and the mountains are active places—the crash of surf, the gurgling of streams, the swaying of trees bending in the wind. There is such a teeming of life that you want to be a part of it, to investigate the scuttling of hermit crabs in a tide pool, or to savor the individual loveliness of the myriad flowers in an alpine meadow.

By contrast, the desert invites contemplation. Its appeal is less obvious than that of the shore or of a mountain lake. Its fiber is not the easy cliche of admiration for classic landscape. It is formed of tougher stuff. At the beach or in a northern hemlock and spruce forest you sense the inexorability of life, but in the desert you discover its tenacity, its capacity for quiet waiting and enduring. The burning lens of the desert clarifies thinking. It forces an inward probing to discover one's own relation to the immensity that lies beyond a man's frail house of flesh and bone and spirit.

You puzzle out where you stand in a way that seldom is necessary in a more gentle, succoring land. The desert is formidable, immense. It restores the sense of awe that somehow has become lost in our present scramble for comfort and knowledge. It stretches the soul.

Mud flats near sand dunes, Death Valley.

Weathered tree in Cottonwood Canyon, Death Valley.

Abandoned mine at Skidoo ruins.

Spring snow below Aguereberry Point, Death Valley.

Bare cottonwood trees at Scotty's Castle.

Mud-washed hill in the Cottonwood Mountains.

Manzanita, desert lily, sacred datura, coyote melon.

Joshua tree at Red Rock Canyon.

Snow on the east slope of the Tehachapi Mountains.

Joshua Tree National Monument.

Granite boulders, Joshua Tree National Monument.

Fields of granite, Joshua Tree National Monument.

Cholla cactus garden, Joshua Tree National Monument.

Paloverde and smoke tree in Palo Verde Wash, Anza-Borrego.

Borrego Badlands. □ Cholla in Anza-Borrego Desert State Park.

Sand storm in Anza-Borrego.

Wall of rock, Canyon Sin Nombre, Anza-Borrego.

Blistered mud patterns, Carrizo Wash, Anza-Borrego. ☐ Buckhorn cholla cactus at sunrise, Anza-Borrego.

Cholla. □ Desert road through Sheep Hole Mountains.

Amboy Crater and lava flow.

Creosote bush in the Chocolate Mountains, Imperial County.

Interior of the Mitchell Caverns, Providence Mountains.

Mojave prickly pear, Providence Mountains.

Snow geese in flight at Salton Sea National Wildlife Refuge.

Sierra Nevada Mountains from Owens Valley.

Alabama Hills near Lone Pine.

Sierra Nevada Mountains from desert floor.

156

Joshua tree fruit, Tehachapi Mountains.

Rock and sand in the dry Soda Lake at Razor.

Old man cactus, Providence Mountains.

Painted lady butterfly on a Mojave aster.

Chalfant petroglyphs, Owens Valley, north of Bishop.

Bristlecone pine in the White Mountains.

A slope of bristlecone pine cones.

Bloom of a hedgehog cactus.

Plateau on the Nevada side of Death Valley.

Paintbrush in the Inyo Mountains.

Old church in Bodie.

Sand dunes near Stove Pipe Wells, Death Valley.

Salt flats in Death Valley National Monument.

Weather-worn marble, Death Valley. □ Mosaic marble, Mosaic Canyon, Death Valley.

Mosaic Canyon, Death Valley National Monument.

North end of Death Valley to Cottonwood Mountains.

Flower-covered floor of Death Valley.

Mud wash at Zabriskie Point.

Joshua trees against the Tehachapi Mountains at Mojave.

Red Rock Canyon north of Mojave.

Yucca in bloom, foothills of the San Gabriel Mountains.

Clouds over Antelope Valley.

Date palm in a grove, Imperial Valley.

Ocotillo cactus at the base of a hill of gravel, the Anza-Borrego desert.

Smoke tree in the Anza-Borrego Desert.

Desert bighorn sheep in the Living Desert Reserve, Palm Desert.

Barrel cactus bloom, ocotillo bloom, juniper berries, creosote bush bloom.

Fruit of the Joshua tree.

Jet stream over the Mojave Desert.

Saguaro cactus, above Parker Dam on the Colorado River.

Sand dunes of the Colorado Desert at Glamis.

Wild burro in the Whipple Mountains.

Sunset in the Mojave Canyon, Colorado Desert.

Saline backwater of Lake Havasu, Colorado River.

Picacho Mountains north of Fort Yuma Indian Reservation.

Pinnacles on Picacho Peak, Colorado Desert.

Prickly poppy in the Colorado Desert.

Cholla and barrel cactus in the foothills of the Whipple Mountains.

Picacho Peak, southern Colorado Desert.

Desert mariposa, Providence Mountains.

Calico Mountains northeast of Barstow.

Mojave prickly pear, Providence Mountains.

Spring snow in Gold Valley, Providence Mountains. □ Soda Lake Basin south of Baker.

Titus Canyon, Death Valley National Monument. ☐ Ash-covered basin at Ubehebe Crater, Death Valley.